Math Sponges
enriching ways to soak up spare moments

US SOAK

Leigh Childs
Nancy Adams

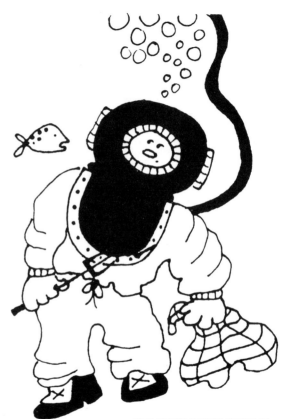

Illustrations: Dianne Truett
Calligraphy: Nancy Schwartz

ISBN 0-86651-248-9

Order number DS01506

DALE
SEYMOUR
PUBLICATIONS
P.O. BOX 10888
PALO ALTO, CA 94303

12 13 14 15 16 17 18-DR-00 99 98 97

Acknowledgements

Idea

MADELINE HUNTER

principal of University Elementary School, U.C.L.A.

Support

CAROL WINNER

president of N.I.C.E.

Art

DIANNE TRUETT

whose drawings translate the "fun of sponging"

far better than words

SUGGESTIONS FOR SPONGING

USE SPONGES to...

- focus the groups attention
- build readiness
- practice for fluency
- review or extend previous learning
- fill spare moments

These activities are intended for intensive classroom use, and are organized simply to save your time. A SUBJECT INDEX is included for convenience, but remember that most sponges are adaptable to a wide variety of skills and ability levels. (Alter these sponges to suit your classroom.) Whenever possible we have included VARIATIONS (rule changes, ways to simplify or add complexity) and EXTENSIONS (ways to extend into higher level thinking).

An ARROW indicates there is more information on the reverse side of the card. You will find additional suggestions, examples, and applications. (You might even find some answers.)

It is our hope that "sponging" will build enthusiasm for math in your classroom. As soon as you establish the "sponging habit," you will find your students eager to repeat their favorites. Encourage them to write their own problems, examples, patterns, and variations. Sponges are for everyone to share and enjoy. Once a particular sponge is understood, your students will want to lead the activity. This increased participation builds self-concept and strengthens positive feelings for math. (It also affords you a few free moments.)

Happy Sponging ...

CONTENTS

TOPIC INDEX

BASIC FACTS

1 Addition Trails
3 Antenna Arithmetic
5 Beanbag Toss
10 Connecting Squares
12 Disappearing Man
14 Drill Bingo
15 Equation Formulation
16 Fast Math
19 Geo-Addition
20 Geometric Designs
23 Living Math
25 Math Match
30 Operation Arrays
31 Operation Relations
35 Position Problems
36 Rhythm Multiplication
38 Signal Math
39 Silent Math
43 Tic Tac Toe
44 Today's Number
48 What's Left?
50 What's My Rule?

COMPUTATION

1 Addition Trails
2 Alphabet Math
6 Be the Teacher
7 Brilliant Teacher
16 Fast Math
18 Game of Checks
19 Geo-Addition
22 Honeycomb Subtraction
27 Menu Math
29 Name the Coins
33 Picture Problems
35 Position Problems
39 Silent Math
44 Today's Number

COUNTING & NUMBER FAMILIARITY

8 Chalk Talk
11 Counting to 21
12 Disappearing Man
17 Find My Number
23 Living Math
25 Math Match
26 Memory Math
28 Name that Pattern
37 Shapes
40 Skip Counting
42 Three in a Row
46 What Belongs?
48 What's Left?
51 What's Next?
52 Which Doesn't Belong?

GRAPHING COORDINATES

4 Anti-Tic Tac Toe
34 Plick Plack Plot

LOGIC & PATTERNS

4 Anti-Tic Tac Toe
7 Brilliant Teacher
9 Change Shaker
10 Connecting Squares
11 Counting to 21
21 Hang in There
28 Name that Pattern
34 Plick Plack Plot
46 What Belongs?
48 What's Left?
49 What's My Number?
50 What's My Rule?
51 What's Next?
52 Which Doesn't Belong?

MONEY

2 Alphabet Math
9 Change Shaker
13 Dollar Dash
27 Menu Math
29 Name the Coins

NUMBERS IN THE REAL WORLD

2 Alphabet Math
23 Living Math
24 Math Bug
27 Menu Math
29 Name the Coins
32 Personal Numbers
33 Picture Problems
38 Signal Math
41 The Clock Strikes
42 Three in a Row
44 Today's Number

PLACE VALUE

13 Dollar Dash
21 Hang in There
49 What's My Number?

SHAPE FAMILIARITY

8 Chalk Talk
17 Find My Number
19 Geo-Addition
20 Geometric Designs
37 Shapes
45 What Am I?
47 What's in a Name?

ADDITION TRAILS

purpose: Practice addition

prep: Make a chart that allows the target number to be changed.

procedure: Students take turns showing a "trail" that will correctly end with the sum shown in the bottom square.

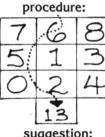

The trail finder puts a new number in the bottom square and calls on a peer to draw the right trail.

suggestion: Use a transparency or laminated chart that allows trails to be erased and the total easily changed.

variations: Allow addition and subtraction trails.

INCREASE DIFFICULTY -- Use a 4 x 4 grid with an adjoining sum square.

Sample 4 x 4 grid:

3	7	1	6
5	2	4	0
3	6	5	7
0	1	2	4

16

Solution trails:

3	7	1	6
5	2	4	0
3	6	5	7
0	1	2	4

16

ALPHABET MATH

purpose: Practice addition

prep: Make a code chart.

procedure: Display a code which assigns monetary value to the alphabet. (The letter A is worth 1¢, B=2¢ ...Z=26¢.)

Children use the code to give values to words.

Sample questions:

"What is the value of your first name?"
"How much is TUESDAY worth?"
"Which is worth more: TEN or THREE?"

variation: SIMPLIFY -- Limit the range to 1 - 5¢ and repeat 5 times.

extension: CHALLENGE your students with a few of these:

"Can you find a word worth a quarter?"

"What is the difference between the values of your first and last names?"

TEAM ACTIVITIES:

"Which person on your team has the most expensive name?"

"How many words can you find that are worth more than MATH?"

"Try to find a word worth a dollar."

"You have three minutes to see how many words you can find that are worth more than a quarter but less than a half dollar."

ANTENNA ARITHMETIC

purpose: Practice basic facts

prep: Draw matrix with numbers.
Prepare appropriate problems.
(If desired, make cards.)

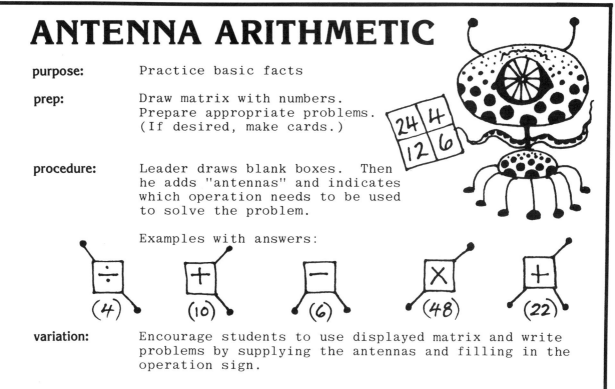

procedure: Leader draws blank boxes. Then
he adds "antennas" and indicates
which operation needs to be used
to solve the problem.

Examples with answers:

variation: Encourage students to use displayed matrix and write
problems by supplying the antennas and filling in the
operation sign.

3

ANTI-TIC TAC TOE

purpose: Practice plotting coordinates

prep: Draw a 4 x 4 grid (with or without numbers)

procedure:

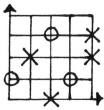

This challenging TEAM game is similar to "Plick Plack Plot" (Sponge # **34**) but now each team wants to AVOID getting three marks in a row.

Divide the group into two teams. The teams take turns calling and plotting coordinates until one team is forced into making three in a row. That team loses.

suggestions: For frequent use, make a 4 x 4 grid transparency or a laminated chart.

Use a 3 x 3 grid for a faster game.

4

Game near completion:

(Solid marks have been
plotted previously.)

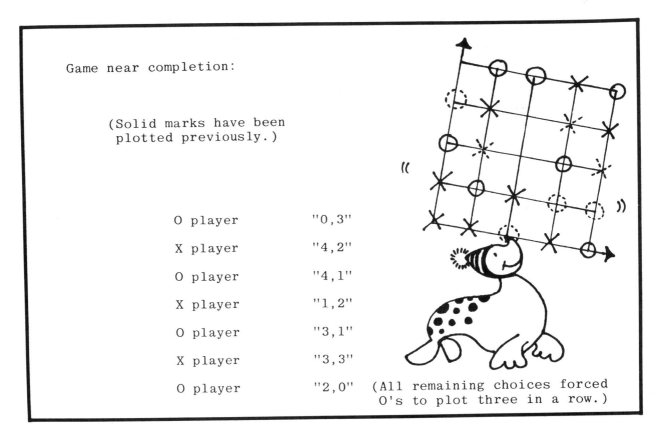

O player	"0,3"
X player	"4,2"
O player	"4,1"
X player	"1,2"
O player	"3,1"
X player	"3,3"
O player	"2,0"

(All remaining choices forced
O's to plot three in a row.)

BEANBAG TOSS

purpose: Practice basic facts

prep: None
(Need: a beanbag
   or a ball)

procedure: Group stands or sits
in a circle. Leader
states a problem and
tosses the beanbag to
a child. The child must answer the problem before
tossing the beanbag back to the teacher.

variations: INCREASE DIFFICULTY -- After answering the leader's
problem, the catcher makes up another problem. (The
beanbag is then tossed from child to child.)

HARDER STILL -- Try to see if the children can answer
the problem BEFORE catching the beanbag.

BE THE TEACHER

purpose: Practice computation skills

prep: None
(If desired, make cards.)

procedure: Display a math problem.
Students decide if the
answer is correct or incorrect.

If there's an error, the children try to identify
exactly where and how it occurred.

variation: This activity has many possible applications.

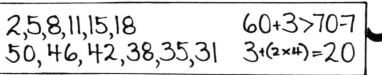

6

Samples of problems with errors:

```
   62          436          164
 + 28        + 356           36
 ────        ─────           14
   81          882        + 255
                           ─────
                             468


   32          425          500
 - 18        - 266        - 246
 ────        ─────        ─────
   26          269          264


   34          726              82
 ×  6        ×   5          8)6506
 ────        ─────            64
 1824         4550            ──
                              16
                              16
                              ──
```

BRILLIANT TEACHER

purpose: Practice addition

prep: None

procedure: Follow these steps:

1 Ask a child to state any 3-digit number.
2 Write it on the board.
3 YOU add the next 3-digit number so that the total is 999.
4 Repeat this procedure.
5 Call on another child to add the last 3-digit number.
6 YOU write in the answer and walk away from the board looking very smug.

```
  5 8 7
  4 1 2
  6 9 3
  3 0 6
  4 1 8
  ─────
2 4 1 6
```

suggestion: Repeat this activity without explanation so the children can discover the procedure on their own.

7

Sample activity:

First child states:	234
Teacher adds:	765
Second child states:	888
Teacher adds:	111
Last child states:	765
Teacher writes answer:	2763

warning: Reject 9's in the hundreds place. If a child offers
a 900 number, just ask him to choose another number.

hint: The answer is always the last number minus 2 plus 2000.

CHALK TALK

purpose: Recognize shapes and increase listening skills

prep: None

procedure: Children sit with their backs to the chalkboard and cover their eyes.

Teacher draws a shape on the chalkboard SLOWLY and DELIBERATELY. The children try to guess what was drawn by the sounds they heard as the shape was drawn.

suggestion: Let the children draw shapes also.

variation: This sponge can be used for number and letter recognition.

CHANGE SHAKER

purpose: Reinforce understanding of coins and their values

prep: Place some coins in a small container. Make 20 tally marks on the board.

procedure: Shake the container.

Using the "20 Questions" format, children try to determine what coins are in the container and their total value.

Erase one tally mark for each question asked.

Sample questions: "Do you have any nickels?"
"Are the coins worth more than 50¢?"

variations: SIMPLIFY -- Allow only 2 or 3 types of coins.

Place a DOMINO in a container and have children try to identify it.

9

Sample game:

Guessers	Response
"Are your coins worth more than 30¢?"	"No"
"Are the coins worth more than 20¢?"	"Yes"
"Are your coins worth less than 25¢?"	"Yes"
"Are they worth less than 23¢?"	"No"
"Do the coins equal 24¢?" (They could be worth 23¢.)	"Yes"
"Do you have any dimes?"	"No"
"Do you have 4 nickels and 4 pennies?"	"YES!"

CONNECTING SQUARES

purpose: Develop strategy skills

prep: Draw playing grid. If students are to play with a partner, provide scratch paper.

procedure: Divide the group into two teams.

Teams take turns drawing a straight line from the center of one square to the center of an adjoining square. The line must start and end on an unused square and cannot cross an existing line.

The team who draws the last possible line wins.

variations: Play more than one game and each winning team's score is the sum of the remaining numbers.

FACTS PRACTICE -- Player must give the sum, product, or difference of the two connected numbers to draw line.

variation: INCREASE DIFFICULTY by making the playing grid 4 x 4 or larger.

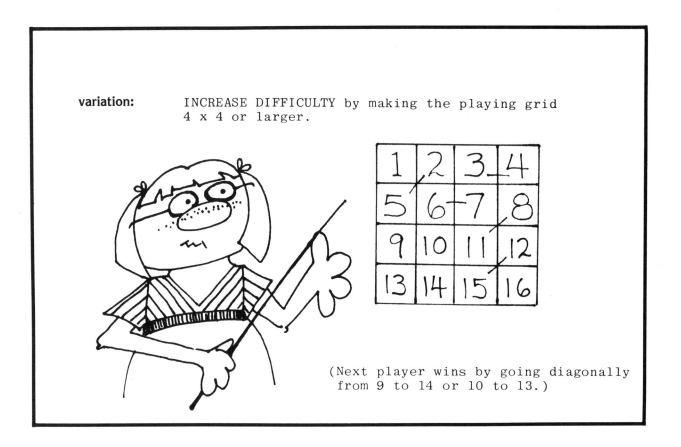

(Next player wins by going diagonally from 9 to 14 or 10 to 13.)

COUNTING TO 21

purpose: Develop strategy skills

prep: None

procedure: This is a counting game played in pairs. The players count consecutively to 21. One or two numbers can be stated on each turn. (The first person says 1, or 1,2 and the other player can say 3, or 3,4 and so on.) The winner is the player who says, "21."

suggestion: This sponge is particularly good as a reward for a productive work period.

variation: Change target number to 15 or 30. Each player can count as many as three numbers on each turn.

Have threesomes play.

DISAPPEARING MAN

purpose: Practice basic facts and numeration skills

prep: Draw a similar geometric man on the chalkboard. Fill in body parts with desired numbers.

procedure: Each child must give an equation (or number situation) equaling a number on the man's body in order to erase that portion of his body.

Sample student responses:

"The next number in the sequence 2,4,6,__."
"What 6 and 3 make."
"The difference between 12 and 8."
"The next odd number after 9."

suggestion: USE SOON. This is a FAVORITE with our students.

variation: Use this sponge for number or letter recognition.

12

Here are some other ideas for drawing a "Disappearing Man."

DOLLAR DASH

purpose: Recognize and write dollars and cents

prep: Make a set of 14 cards - 1-9, two 0's, dollar sign, decimal point and comma (optional).

procedure: Cards are distributed to students.

Leader calls out an amount like "$3.50." Students holding the required cards must arrange themselves in order to correctly show the amount.

variation: TEAM GAME -- Play "Dollar Dash" as a team relay race. (This would require 2 sets of cards.)

extensions: After displaying an amount, ask students to increase that amount by $2.00 ... 50¢ ... 15¢.

Have displaying group rearrange themselves to show the largest possible amount.

See "Menu Math" (Sponge # **27**).

13

DRILL BINGO

purpose: Practice basic facts

prep: (Need: scratch paper and 2 dice, or 2-12 addition flashcards)

procedure: Students make a 5 x 5 grid.

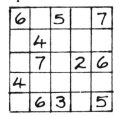

They fill in their grid randomly with the numbers 2 through 12.

Leader rolls dice and announces the numbers rolled. Each player crosses out one number on his playing grid that matches the sum of the two numbers. (If 3 and 5 are rolled each player crosses out one 8.)

Play continues until a player has crossed out 5 in a row in any direction.

suggestion: Guide students as they fill in sums so they include only one or two 2's, 3's, 11's and 12's.

14

variations: FASTER game -- Use a 3 x 3 or 4 x 4 grid.

To practice HIGHER SUMS -- Use 3 dice and fill in the grid with numbers 3 through 18.

Use SUBTRACTION or DIVISION flashcards and have the students fill in grid with numbers 2 through 9.

For a LONGER game continue until all players have at least one "Bingo." Players total their 5 "Bingo" numbers and the one with the highest (or lowest) total is the winner.

EQUATION FORMULATION

purpose: Practice basic facts

prep: None
(Need: paper)

procedure: Draw 10 numbers and a few math symbols on the chalkboard.

Allow 2-3 minutes for the children to form as many equations as possible.

Examples:

$$5-3=2 \qquad 4 \times 5 = 20 \qquad 3 \times 6 + 2 = 20$$
$$10 + 5 = 15 \qquad 20 \div 5 > 3 \qquad 20 \div 5 = 10 - 6$$

variation: Name a particular sum or product and let the children BRAINSTORM ways to arrive at that number.

Example: Using 3 numbers, how many ways can you make 24?

15

extension: Require a specific number of operations.

Example:

"Using these numbers and symbols, make equations that add, multiply, and subtract in that order."

$2 + 3 \times 5 - 8 = 17$

FAST MATH

purpose: Practice computation skills

prep: None

procedure: Teacher gives verbal on-going problem and the children try to keep up with the answer.

> Example: "Start with 6... Square it... Subtract 1... Divide by 7... Multiply it by 9...... Where are we now?"

suggestion: This sponge is an excellent warm up drill for the upper grades.

variation: "SLOW MATH" -- Use a slower pace and smaller numbers.

> Example: "1 plus 2 plus 3 plus 4 minus 3..."

16

FIND MY NUMBER

purpose: Integrate use of directional words with number concepts

prep: Make chart with shape and numbers.

procedure: Display chart.

Leader selects one of the numbers and gives verbal clues.

Example: "My number is inside the triangle."
"It's an odd number."
"It's in a corner."

Student who identifies the number gets to be the new leader.

suggestion: Ideal FLANNELBOARD ACTIVITY which increases application possibilities.

17

GAME OF CHECKS

purpose: Practice addition

prep: (Need: scratch paper)

procedure: Draw recording chart.

Students find many ways to express a particular sum.

Example: "Find ways to make 25."

16	8	4	2	1
✓		✓	✓✓	✓
	✓✓✓			✓
	✓✓	✓✓		✓

suggestion: Conclude activity with questions based on the group's findings. "Which solution used 6 checks?" "Which way used the least number of checks?"

variations: Limit the number of checks allowed in any one box.

Apply this activity to MONEY and make a coin chart.

18

variations: TIMED ACTIVITY -- Group sees how many different solutions they can make in 5 minutes.

Sample chart for "Money variation:"

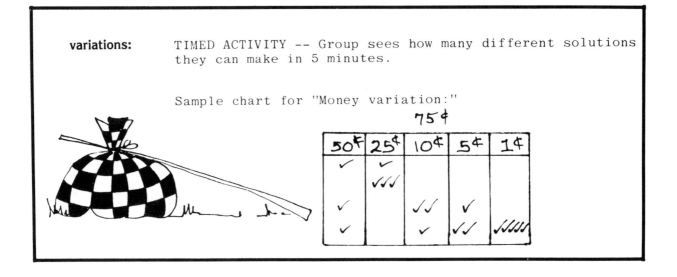

75¢

50¢	25¢	10¢	5¢	1¢
✓	✓			
	✓✓✓			
✓		✓✓	✓	
✓		✓	✓✓	/////

GEO-ADDITION

purpose: Practice addition facts and increase familiarity of geometric shapes

prep: None

procedure: Students are to find the total numerical value of each series of geometric shapes by finding the sum of all the sides of each shape in the series.

Examples:

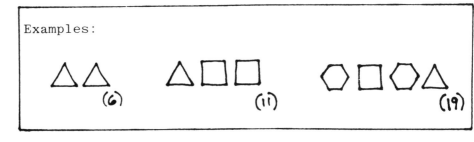

(6)

(11)

(19)

19

More examples:

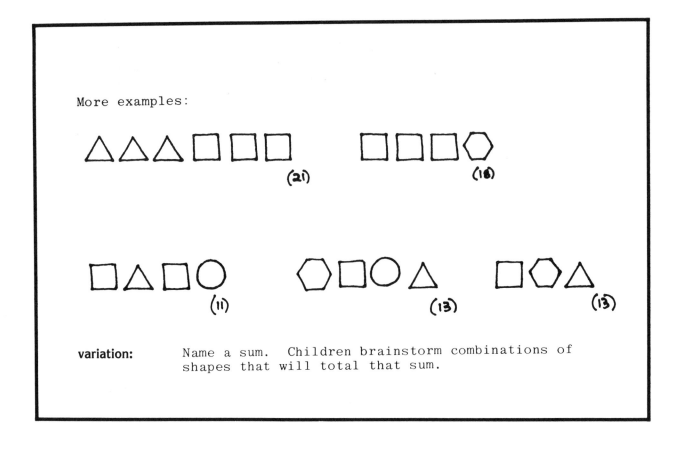

△△△□□□
(21)

□□□⬡
(16)

□△□○
(11)

⬡□○△
(13)

□⬡△
(13)

variation: Name a sum. Children brainstorm combinations of
shapes that will total that sum.

GEOMETRIC DESIGNS

purpose: Increase familiarity with shapes and practice addition facts

prep: Display shapes with different numerical values.
(If desired, make cards.)

procedure: Review shape names by asking questions such as, "Which shape is worth 4? Which shape is one less than 3?"

Make a drawing using the displayed geometric shapes. Students determine the value of your drawing.

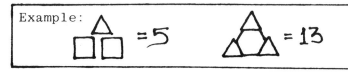

variation: Make shapes worth monetary values.

extensions:

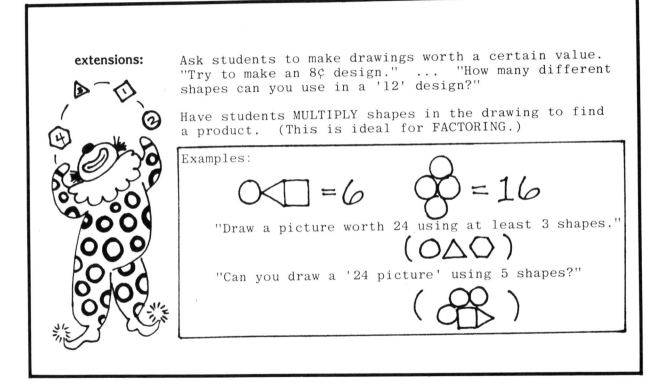

Ask students to make drawings worth a certain value.
"Try to make an 8¢ design." ... "How many different
shapes can you use in a '12' design?"

Have students MULTIPLY shapes in the drawing to find
a product. (This is ideal for FACTORING.)

Examples:

"Draw a picture worth 24 using at least 3 shapes."

"Can you draw a '24 picture' using 5 shapes?"

HANG IN THERE

purpose: Reinforce understanding of place value and develop strategy skills

prep: Draw chart for recording guesses.

procedure: Leader thinks of a 2-place number. (Avoid repeating digits, like 33.)

Group tries to guess the number by stating a 2-place number. Leader responds by placing the guessed number in the appropriate column.

Hang in There means a numeral is in the number but in the wrong place.

Right On means a numeral is properly placed.

No means neither numeral is in the number.

Game continues until someone guesses the number.

21

suggestion:

SIMPLIFY -- Avoid numbers with zero. Later when using zeros remind the students that in a 1-digit number, zero is understood to be in the ten's place.

extension:

Play game with 3-place numbers and only provide verbal feedback.

Example of a game (target number is 438):

Guesses	Responses
821	"Hang in there, No, No"
796	"No, No, No."
584	"No, Hang in there, Hang in there."
408	"Right on, No, Right on."
438	"That's it."

HONEYCOMB SUBTRACTION

purpose: Practice subtraction

prep: Draw honeycomb arrangement and hexagon key. Fill in top number.

procedure: Students use the hexagon key to determine how to fill in the missing numbers.

Change top number to reuse chart and continue practice.

variations: SIMPLIFY activity by making a hexagon key with lower numbers.

INCREASE DIFFICULTY with a -7, -8, -9 key.

extension: Have students discover different honeycomb arrangements (hexagon designs) and make a hexagon key that will work.

22

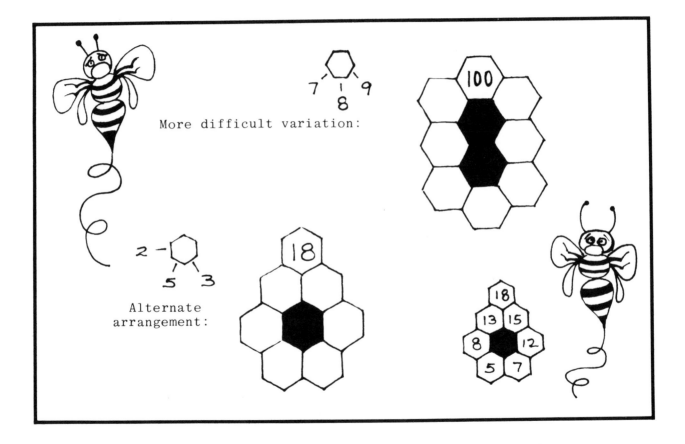

More difficult variation:

Alternate arrangement:

LIVING MATH

purpose: Practice forming equations

prep: Make large numeral cards (0 through 18) and symbol cards (+ - =).

procedure: Call out 2 numbers that are to be added (or subtracted).
Children with the required numbers and symbols arrange themselves to correctly show the complete equation.

> Example: "Subtract 8 from 11."

variation: Include the inequality signs **>** and **<**.

extension: Give a word problem. Children form the math equation that illustrates and answers the problem.

Example: "Susan invited 11 friends to her party. 8 children have arrived. How many are missing?"

23

MATH BUG

purpose: Practice spelling math words

prep: None

procedure: This game is played like "Hangman," but only math-related words are used.

Instead of a "hangman," use a MATH BUG. For each guessed letter that is not in the target word, erase one part of the bug.

suggestion: Ask a student volunteer to draw a math bug on the board.

variation: This sponge can easily be a TEAM GAME, or a "pairs activity" on rainy days.

MATH MATCH

purpose: Improve memory and practice basic facts

prep: Make a 4 x 4 playing grid with 8 pairs. Need: 16 thick covers

procedure: Display grid with each space covered.

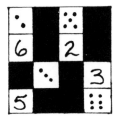

Students take turns uncovering two spaces. If they get a match, they keep the 2 covers and get another turn. If the spaces do not match, they are recovered and another student gets a turn.

Continue playing until all pairs are matched.

suggestion: To encourage more participation, limit number of pairs a player may take.

INTRODUCE activity with a matching colors or shapes game. Then match math equations and answers.

variations:

CARD GAME -- For a small group use 20 cards (10 pairs) which are arranged face down and turned over as each child takes a turn.

Suggested sequence for INCREASING DIFFICULTY:

$2+3$ & 5 → $6+6$ & $4+8$ → $15-8$ & $4+3$
$3×6$ & $2×9$ → $12-4$ & $24÷3$

INCREASE DIFFICULTY by enlarging size of grid to 4 x 5, 6 x 5 or 6 x 6.

Other possible applications:

Match math symbols to their meaning
$>$ & greater than

Match equivalent measures
7 days & 1 week   3 feet & 1 yard

Match equivalent fractions (or to decimals)
3/4 & 9/12   2/5 & 40%

MEMORY MATH

purpose: Improve memory and practice
number recognition

prep: None

procedure: Display 4 numbers.

Students look the other way while
you erase one of the numbers.

Then they turn around and try to determine which
number is missing.

suggestion: Verbalize the numbers with the children before asking
them to look away.

variations: SIMPLIFY -- Arrange the numbers numerically.

INCREASE DIFFICULTY -- Include more and higher numbers.

To practice number patterns, erase one of the numbers
in a pattern.

MENU MATH

purpose: Practice solving story
                 problems involving money

prep: None
                 (Need: menus)

procedure: Display menu.

> Teacher asks simple story problems
> which require children to refer to
> the menu to solve the problems.
>
> If you have 3 quarters & 2 nickels
> could you buy a pink surprise ?

extensions: Use menus with "Dollar Dash" (Sponge # 13). Call out
                 an item. Children holding cards must arrange themselves
                 to correctly show the proper price.

                 HARDER STILL -- Ask the children to make up their own
                 story problems. The card holders solve and show the
                 answer.

27

SUNDAES

SEAL SHERBERT SUNDAE....$1.10
sherbert & pineapples

SCOOTER SUNDAE....$.75
chocolate & whipped cream

ROCKY RACOON SUNDAE....$.95
rocky road and marshmallows

SURPRISE.............$.85

THE PINK
vanilla and strawberries

BANANA SPLIT...$1.50
chocolate and vanilla with bananas

EXTRA NUTS........$.15

EXTRA WHIPPED CREAM.....$.10

CONES
TRIPLE.....$.60
DOUBLE...$.40
SINGLE...$.25
1 scoop-cup... $.30

YUM

NAME THAT PATTERN

purpose: Predict patterns

prep: Make pattern strips and put them into a container which allows for partial removal and display of the patterns.

procedure: Students try to name a pattern in as few clues as possible. This is a team game with a format like the TV show, "Name That Tune." Teams compete for a chance to predict the pattern. ("We can name that pattern in 6 clues." "We can name it in just 5 clues.")

Sample patterns:

●○○●○__   1,4,7,10,__   △2□4△6□8__

suggestions: Use 7 as a starting point. Teams decrease the number of clues from there.

Use student authored clues.

28

More patterns:

6, 12, 18, 24, ...
50, 46, 42, 38, ...
1, 2, 4, 8, 16, ...

Challenging patterns:

Z, 12, Y, 14, X, 12, ...
10, 9, 14, 13, 18, 17, ...
212, 323, 434, ...
975, 864, 753, ...

NAME THE COINS

purpose: Reinforce understanding of coins and their values

prep: Place coins in a small container

procedure: Divide group into two teams.

Shake the container and announce the total value of the coins.

Example: "These coins total 51¢."

Teams take turns guessing what coins might be inside. One point is scored by a team if they give a new combination that equals the same value. Three points are awarded to a team that identifies the coins exactly.

suggestion: Use a feedback form similar to that shown above so the students know what's already been guessed.

extension: See "Change Shaker" (Sponge # 9).

29

OPERATION ARRAYS

purpose: Increase familiarity with number relationships and practice all operations

prep: Make an operation array chart which allows numbers to be easily changed. Fill in the numbers.

procedure: Students study chart. They decide which operation signs $+ - \times \div$ will correctly complete the equation in each row and column. Fill in the operation sign as each equation is solved.

variation: TEAM ACTIVITY -- Make 2 copies of the operation array. Teams together fill in the missing operation signs. One point is earned for each correct row or column. The first team finished receives two points.

extension: Have the students author operation arrays for their classmates to solve.

One solution:

16	−	8	−	3	=	5
÷		÷		×		×
4	−	2	×	1	=	2
×		÷		+		−
3	+	4	−	3	=	4
=		=		=		=
12	×	1	−	6	=	6

More examples:

1		6		2	=	3
9		2		8	=	3
5		3		2	=	6
=		=		=		=
5		6		8	=	3

5		6		3	=	10
9		6		3	=	6
7		7		2	=	2
=		=		=		=
2		7		3	=	6

OPERATION RELATIONS

purpose: Practice basic facts and understand relationships

prep: None
(Need: paper)

procedure: Ask the students to write one math problem on a piece of paper.

> Write the following statements on the chalkboard:
>
> ___ is greater than ___
> ___ is equal to ___
> ___ is less than ___

One child holds up a problem and chooses another child to hold up a problem. The two children must hold their problems in the proper place on the chalkboard in order to make a true statement.

➡

variations:

SIMPLIFY -- Teacher writes in a number after a statement, and the children hold up problems that fit.

_____ is greater than 6

Compare fractional numbers.

$\frac{3}{8}$ is less than $\frac{1}{2}$

extension:

Write additional statements on the chalkboard.

_____ is 2 more than _____

_____ is 5 more than _____

PERSONAL NUMBERS

126

purpose: Increase awareness of numbers in the real world

prep: None
(Need: scratch paper)

procedure: Allow 2 or 3 minutes for students to write down numbers that are somehow related to them.

Ask a volunteer to share a number aloud. The group tries to guess how that number is related to the volunteer.

Example: "MY PERSONAL NUMBER IS 126."

Possible guesses: IS IT YOUR ... BIRTHDAY?
... ADDRESS NUMBER?
... PAGE IN YOUR MATH BOOK?
... COMBINED AGES OF YOUR WHOLE FAMILY?

suggestion: This is an effective sponge to try with parents. It illustrates the role parents can play in making math relevant to the child's world outside of the classroom.

More examples:

7829901   (phone number)

8 4 42   (birthday)

12 25   (favorite day of year)

126   (address number)

9 05   (recess time)

563 66 1212   (social security)

PICTURE PROBLEMS

purpose: Practice word problems
and increase awareness
of math in the real world

prep: Select interesting pictures.

procedure: Display a picture.

Ask the children to make up word
problems that go with the picture.

variation: INCREASE DIFFICULTY -- Add number limitations.
("Think of a problem that has an answer of 45.")

HARDER STILL -- Add operation requirements. ("Make
up a story problem which requires division." "Think
of a problem which requires three operations.")

extension: See "Living Math" (Sponge # 23). Children use the
number cards to show the story problem's equation
and answer.

Sample questions:

"How many candles are on the cake?"

"If four candles are blown out, how many
are still left to blow out?"

"How many boys and girls are in this picture?"

"How many more packages are wrapped in patterned
paper than in paper with dots?"

PLICK PLACK PLOT

purpose: Introduce plotting of coordinates

prep: Display a 4 x 4 grid (without numbers) that can be marked.

procedure: Divide group into two teams (X's and O's).

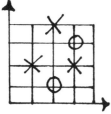

Show grid and explain that the object of the game is to plot three of your team's marks in a row (horizontally, vertically or diagonally).

Ask one person on the "X" team to state two numbers under five. RATHER DELIBERATELY, plot an X on the corresponding coordinate. Continue this procedure, alternating teams, until one team gets three in a row.

suggestion: When students understand how to plot coordinates, require the winning team to have 4 marks in a row. (If time allows, expand grid to 5 x 5.)

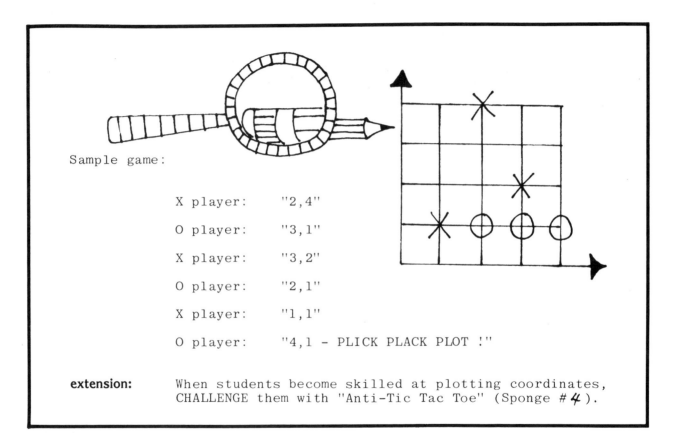

Sample game:

X player:	"2,4"
O player:	"3,1"
X player:	"3,2"
O player:	"2,1"
X player:	"1,1"
O player:	"4,1 - PLICK PLACK PLOT !"

extension: When students become skilled at plotting coordinates, CHALLENGE them with "Anti-Tic Tac Toe" (Sponge # 4).

POSITION PROBLEMS

purpose: Practice basic facts

prep: Make grid and problems that cover desired facts.

procedure: Display grid. Students note position of numbers on grid, and answer problems using position clues.

Examples using illustration above:

$\boxed{5} + \boxed{2} = 7$ $\ulcorner - \urcorner =$ $\sqcap \div \sqcap =$

$\llcorner + \sqcap + \sqsubset =$ $\urcorner \times \ulcorner =$

---

variation: INCREASE DIFFICULTY -- Have students answer problems using the coded symbols.

extension: To include more than 9 numbers, display additional different arrangements.

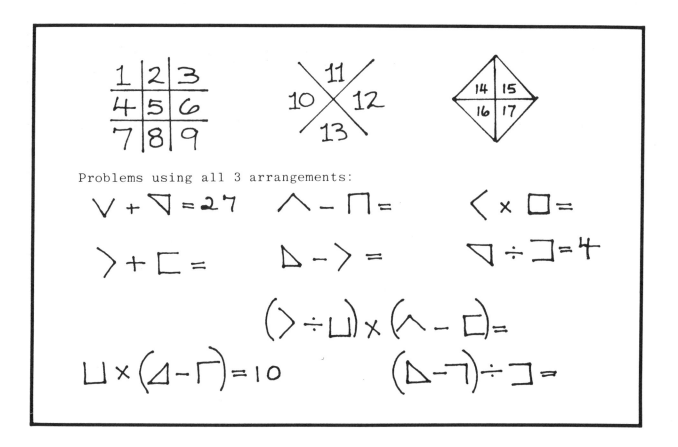

1	2	3
4	5	6
7	8	9

11
10 ╳ 12
13

14 | 15
16 | 17

Problems using all 3 arrangements:

∨ + ◹ = 27   ∧ − ⊓ =   < × □ =

> + ⊏ =   △ − > =   ◹ ÷ ⊐ = 4

(> ÷ ⊔) × (∧ − ⊏) =

⊔ × (△ − ⌐) = 10   (△ − ⌐) ÷ ⊐ =

RHYTHM MULTIPLICATION

purpose: Practice multiplication facts

prep: None

procedure: Group forms a circle. Leader begins a rhythmic sequence (slap slap, clap clap, snap snap). Children join in as they discover the pattern.

When everyone is participating, the leader states a multiplication fact during the "snapping stage." Without interrupting the rhythmic activity, the child to the leader's left responds with the answer at the next "snapping stage." Activity continues clockwise with each child answering a fact posed by the teacher.

The group's GOAL is to go all the way around the circle without breaking the rhythmic pattern.

suggestion: Set a slow pace to allow for greater success.

Sample start:

       Teacher: Slap, slap, clap, clap, "two sevens."

       Child 1:   Slap, slap, clap, clap, "four-teen."

       Teacher: Slap, slap, clap, clap, "four fives."

       Child 2:   Slap, slap, clap, clap, "twen-ty."

variation: INCREASE DIFFICULTY by having responding child pose
the next multiplication problem instead of the leader.

SHAPES

purpose: Increase familiarity with shapes and understanding of numbers

prep: Draw overlapping shapes with numbers.

procedure: Students use drawing to answer the leader's questions.

Sample questions:
"What number is only in the triangle?"
"What number appears inside all 3 shapes?"
"Which number inside the circle is even?"
"What's the largest odd number in the rectangle?"

variation: INCREASE DIFFICULTY -- Put more than one number in each region. Use larger numbers or add another overlapping shape, such as a trapezoid, square, or oval.

More difficult variation:

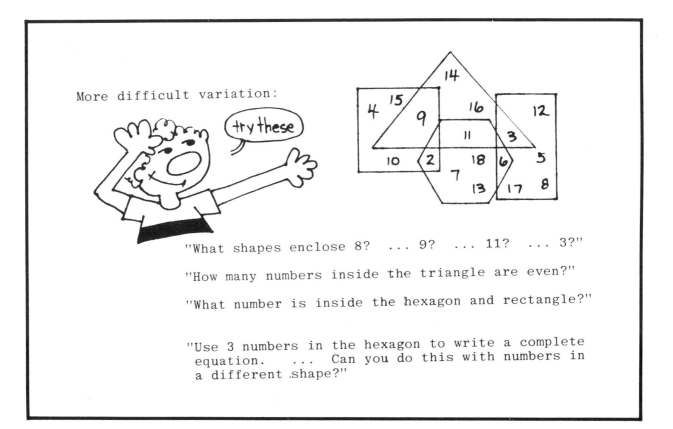

"What shapes enclose 8? ... 9? ... 11? ... 3?"

"How many numbers inside the triangle are even?"

"What number is inside the hexagon and rectangle?"

"Use 3 numbers in the hexagon to write a complete equation. ... Can you do this with numbers in a different shape?"

SIGNAL MATH

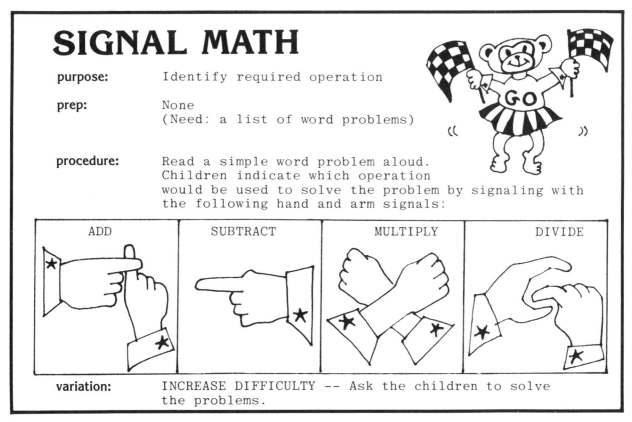

purpose: Identify required operation

prep: None
(Need: a list of word problems)

procedure: Read a simple word problem aloud.
Children indicate which operation
would be used to solve the problem by signaling with
the following hand and arm signals:

ADD	SUBTRACT	MULTIPLY	DIVIDE

variation: INCREASE DIFFICULTY -- Ask the children to solve
the problems.

38

SILENT MATH

purpose: Reinforce computation skills

prep: None

procedure:
NO TALKING IS ALLOWED.
The teacher writes an equation
(without the answer) on the chalkboard.
Chalk is then handed to a volunteer who
completes the equation and writes the next one.

A writes: $6+3=$

B writes: $9 \times 4 =$

C writes: $36-7=$

Activity continues silently as the chalk is handed
around the group.

variations:
SIMPLIFY -- Set a limit to the answer. (40 or 100)

SPIRAL SILENT MATH -- Place a large sheet of paper
on the floor. The group gathers around the paper
and the on-going equation spirals around the paper.

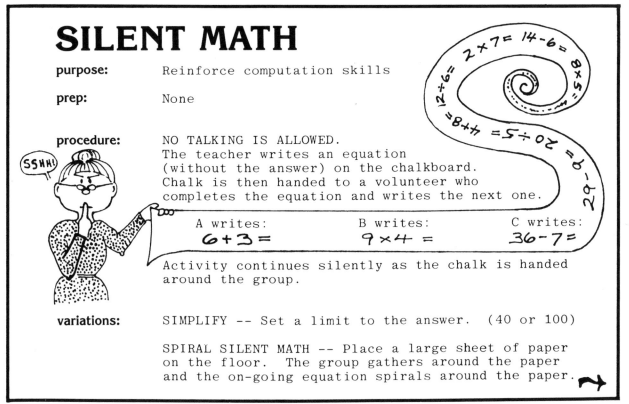

39

SKIP COUNTING

0,3,6,9...

purpose: Increase familiarity with numbers and their order

prep: None

procedure: Leader begins with zero and skip counts by 2's (or 5's, 10's, 3's). As soon as children identify the pattern they join the rhythmic counting aloud.

Example:

0, 3, 6, 9, 15, 18, 21, 24, ...

variations: Start on a different number than zero.

2, 5, 8, 11, 14, 17, 20, ...

INCREASE DIFFICULTY -- skip count backwards.

50, 45, 40, 35, 30, ...

Dramatize this activity by having the group count like a laughing hyena ... an old man ... an opera star.

THE CLOCK STRIKES

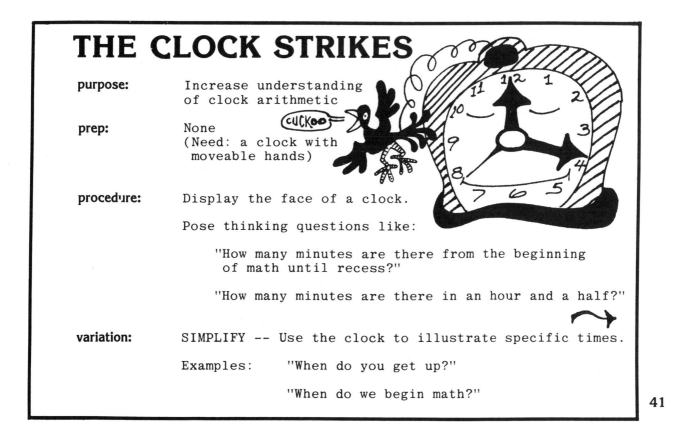

purpose: Increase understanding of clock arithmetic

prep: None
(Need: a clock with moveable hands)

procedure: Display the face of a clock.

Pose thinking questions like:

"How many minutes are there from the beginning of math until recess?"

"How many minutes are there in an hour and a half?"

variation: SIMPLIFY -- Use the clock to illustrate specific times.

Examples: "When do you get up?"

"When do we begin math?"

41

More questions:

"How many hours are we awake if we get up at 7:00 and go to bed at 8:00?"

"If it's 10:00 now, what time will it be 6 hours from now?"

"How many times does the second hand go around in a half an hour?"

"How many 15 minutes are there in an hour?...in an hour and a half?"

"How many minutes are there in one-third of an hour?"

"How many times a day does a clock strike if it strikes only on the hours?...the half-hours?...both?"

THREE IN A ROW

3	9	11
1	5	8
6	4	0

purpose: Increase awareness of numbers in the real world

prep: (Need: scratch paper and 13 cards numbered 0-12)

procedure: Students draw a 3 x 3 grid (or Tic Tac Toe form with a border) and fill it with numbers from 0 to 12. Use a number only once.

Number is picked (perhaps from a jar or bag of numbers) and clue for that number is read.

Object is to cover three is a row. (When one child has a "Bingo" keep game going to see if others can get three in a row before he gets another "Bingo").

suggestion: If time allows, students play until someone covers their whole grid.

Encourage children to contribute new clues.

42

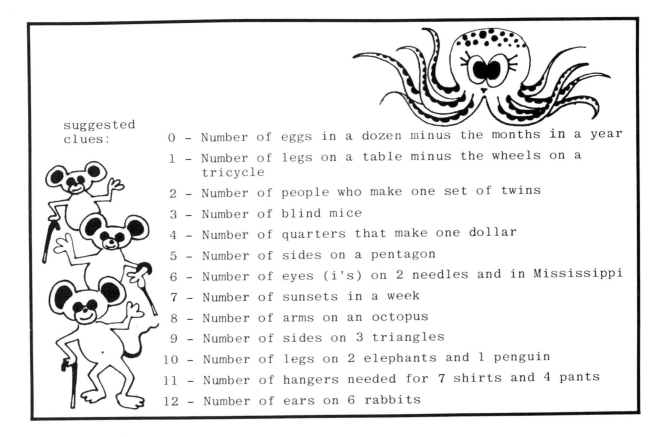

suggested
clues:

0 – Number of eggs in a dozen minus the months in a year

1 – Number of legs on a table minus the wheels on a tricycle

2 – Number of people who make one set of twins

3 – Number of blind mice

4 – Number of quarters that make one dollar

5 – Number of sides on a pentagon

6 – Number of eyes (i's) on 2 needles and in Mississippi

7 – Number of sunsets in a week

8 – Number of arms on an octopus

9 – Number of sides on 3 triangles

10 – Number of legs on 2 elephants and 1 penguin

11 – Number of hangers needed for 7 shirts and 4 pants

12 – Number of ears on 6 rabbits

TIC TAC TOE

purpose: Practice basic facts and increase familiarity with directional words (left, right, top, bottom)

prep: None

procedure: Draw the "Tic Tac Toe" form.

Divide group into two teams (X's and O's).

Leader states a problem. A player on the "X" team gives an answer. If correct, the player tells where he'd like his "X" placed (left, middle). If the answer is incorrect it's the "O's" turn. The teams continue alternating turns, answering problems, and placing their marks until one team has 3 in a row or all 9 spaces are filled.

variation: Use a "Tic Tac Toe" form which includes numbers or equations. Students state a math problem that results in that number.

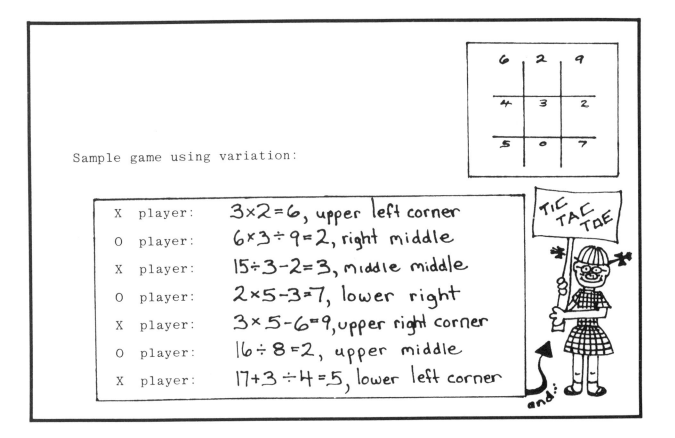

Sample game using variation:

X player:	$3 \times 2 = 6$, upper left corner	
O player:	$6 \times 3 \div 9 = 2$, right middle	
X player:	$15 \div 3 - 2 = 3$, middle middle	
O player:	$2 \times 5 - 3 = 7$, lower right	
X player:	$3 \times 5 - 6 = 9$, upper right corner	
O player:	$16 \div 8 = 2$, upper middle	
X player:	$17 + 3 \div 4 = 5$, lower left corner	

TODAY'S NUMBER

purpose: Practice basic facts and computation skills

prep: None

procedure: On the chalkboard write the day of the month, such as "5" on the fifth of October.

Students think of as many different math problems as they can that result in 5.

Examples:
$$2+3 \qquad 11-6$$
$$30\div6 \qquad 4\times2-3$$

variations: TIMED ACTIVITY -- See how many problems the group can name in 2 minutes. (It's fun to do this a few times during a month and graph the group's results.)

TEAM GAME -- Teams compete to have the most equations. (You might award 2 points for equations using a division sign.)

44

WHAT AM I?

purpose: Practice shape recognition

prep: None

procedure: A child gives a clue about a shape and group guesses the identity of the shape.

> Examples:
> I have three sides. What am I?
> I have four equal sides. What am I?
> I can be drawn without lifting your pencil.

variations: SIMPLIFY -- Use a "20 Questions" format. Leader thinks of a shape and children ask yes/no questions until the shape is identified.

OR, State the name of the shape and the group gives the characteristics of that shape.

> Example: I am a triangle..."You have three sides."

45

WHAT BELONGS?

purpose: Identify and continue patterns

prep: None
(If desired, make cards.)

procedure: Children study drawing. They
try to discover the relationship
of the top two numbers and complete
the missing part so that the bottom
two numbers relate similarly.

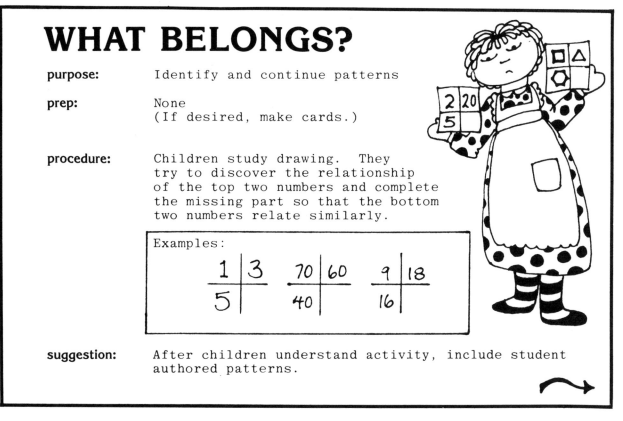

Examples:

1	3
5	

70	60
40	

9	18
16	

suggestion: After children understand activity, include student
authored patterns.

46

More examples:

extension: This sponge easily adapts to other subjects.

WHAT'S IN A NAME?

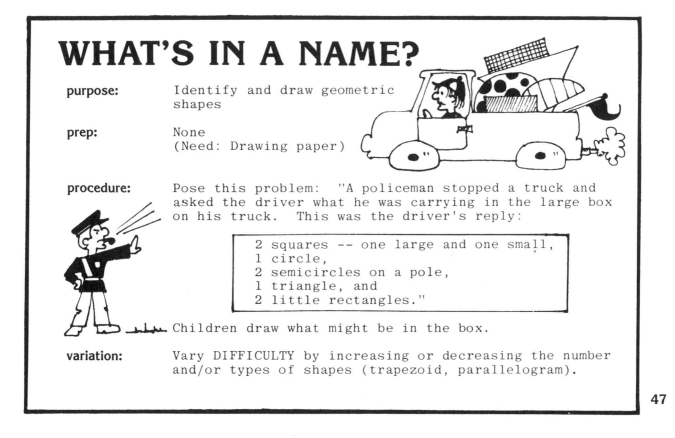

purpose: Identify and draw geometric shapes

prep: None
(Need: Drawing paper)

procedure: Pose this problem: "A policeman stopped a truck and asked the driver what he was carrying in the large box on his truck. This was the driver's reply:

> 2 squares -- one large and one small,
> 1 circle,
> 2 semicircles on a pole,
> 1 triangle, and
> 2 little rectangles."

Children draw what might be in the box.

variation: Vary DIFFICULTY by increasing or decreasing the number and/or types of shapes (trapezoid, parallelogram).

WHAT'S LEFT?

purpose: Practice basic facts and number relationships

prep: Draw and display 3 x 3 grid with numbers. (Need: scratch paper)

procedure: Leader gives clues which eliminate all displayed numbers except one. Students try to identify that mystery number.

Sample game using illustrated grid:

"It's greater than 5.
It's an even number.
It's not 16−8.
What's left?"

variation: INCREASE DIFFICULTY -- Fill grid with the numbers 10 through 18 and give appropriate clues.

48

Another approach using the numbers 1 - 9:

      "Eliminate 2 numbers whose sum is 3.
      Eliminate 2 numbers whose sum is 9.
      Eliminate 2 numbers whose sum is 11.
      Eliminate 2 numbers whose sum is 14.
      What's left?"

                            (... 8)

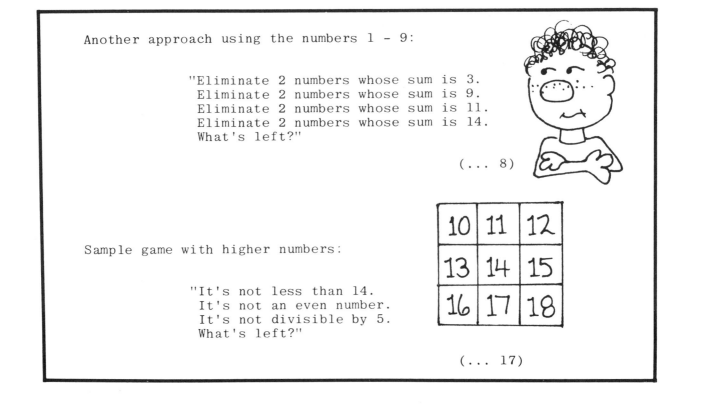

Sample game with higher numbers:

      "It's not less than 14.
      It's not an even number.
      It's not divisible by 5.
      What's left?"

                          (... 17)

10	11	12
13	14	15
16	17	18

WHAT'S MY NUMBER?

purpose: Develop logical thinking skills

prep: None

procedure: Pick a number.

Children ask questions in a "20 Questions" format. The leader responds with non-verbal feedback.

Student who correctly guesses the number selects the next number and gives the non-verbal feedback. (The student may need assistance recording the math symbols.)

> Sample questions and non-verbal feedback:
>
> "Is it 6?" $n \neq 6$
>
> "Is it less than 50?" $n < 50$

variation: TEAM GAME -- Teams score one point for each question asked. The winning team is the one with the lowest score.

49

Sample game:

Questions & Written Feedback

"Is your number less than 50?"	$n > 50$
"Is your number greater than 75?"	$n > 75$
"Is it an even number?"	even
"Is it greater than 85?"	$85 > n$
"Does it have a 7 in it?"	n has a 7
"Is your number 76?"	$n \neq 76$
"Your number is 78!"	you got it!

WHAT'S MY RULE?

purpose: Identify operation and discover patterns

prep: None

procedure: Students study each example to discover the rule and supply the missing number.

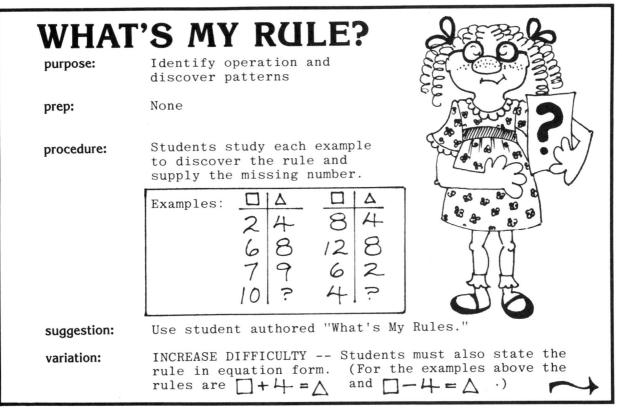

Examples: □	△	□	△
2	4	8	4
6	8	12	8
7	9	6	2
10	?	4	?

suggestion: Use student authored "What's My Rules."

variation: INCREASE DIFFICULTY -- Students must also state the rule in equation form. (For the examples above the rules are $□ + 4 = △$ and $□ - 4 = △$.)

50

More "What's My Rule" examples:

a	b
3	9
4	10
7	13
9	☐

r	s
16	7
13	4
10	1
12	☐

0	☐
3	9
6	36
2	☐

WHAT'S NEXT?

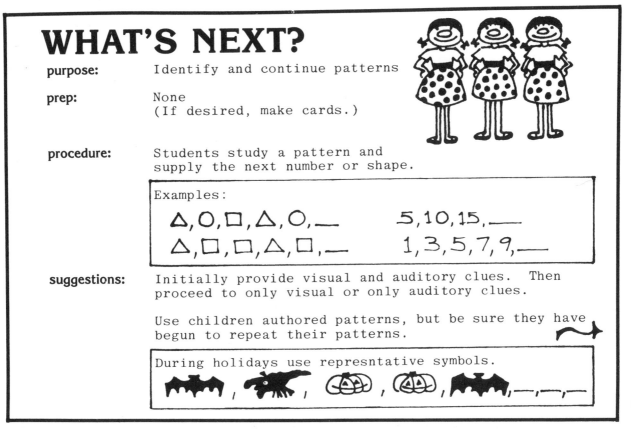

purpose: Identify and continue patterns

prep: None
(If desired, make cards.)

procedure: Students study a pattern and
supply the next number or shape.

Examples:

△, ○, □, △, ○, ___   5, 10, 15, ___

△, □, □, △, □, ___   1, 3, 5, 7, 9, ___

suggestions: Initially provide visual and auditory clues.   Then
proceed to only visual or only auditory clues.

Use children authored patterns, but be sure they have
begun to repeat their patterns.

During holidays use represntative symbols.

51

More examples:

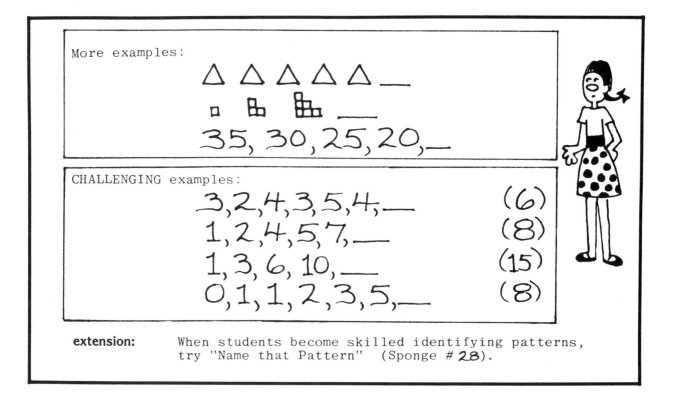

△ △ △ △ △ __

35, 30, 25, 20, __

CHALLENGING examples:

3, 2, 4, 3, 5, 4, __   (6)

1, 2, 4, 5, 7, __   (8)

1, 3, 6, 10, __   (15)

0, 1, 1, 2, 3, 5, __   (8)

extension: When students become skilled identifying patterns, try "Name that Pattern" (Sponge # 28).

WHICH DOESN'T BELONG?

purpose: Discover relationships

prep: None
(If desired, make cards.)

procedure: Students study arrangement. They try to discover how 3 of the 4 numerals (or shapes) are related and which doesn't belong.

When they identify the "misfit" they also explain WHY.

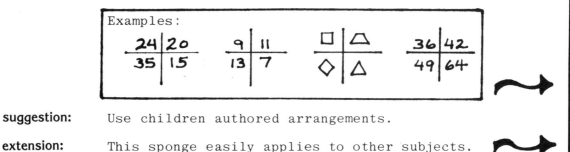

Examples:

24	20
35	15

9	11
13	7

□	△
◇	△

36	42
49	64

suggestion: Use children authored arrangements.

extension: This sponge easily applies to other subjects.

Answers to examples:

24 - Others are divisible by 5.

9 - Others are prime numbers.

△ - Others have 4 sides.

36 - It doesn't have a 4.

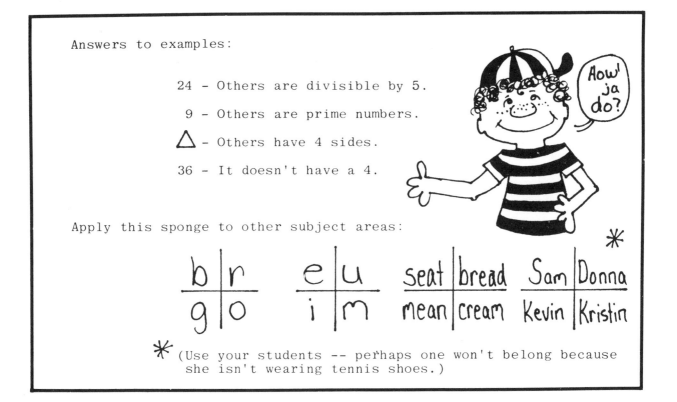

Apply this sponge to other subject areas:

b	r
g	o

e	u
i	m

seat	bread
mean	cream

Sam	Donna
Kevin	Kristin

*

* (Use your students -- perhaps one won't belong because she isn't wearing tennis shoes.)